Order Your Day

Your First 20 Minutes

A Spiritual Perspective

*"The steps of a good man are ordered by the
Lord: and he delighteth in his way."*
Psalm 37:23

W. A. Simmons

Order Your Day

Unless otherwise noted, all scripture references are from the King James Version of the Bible.

ISBN 978-0-9828242-6-9

Cover clock image: © Ivanbogun | Dreamstime.com
Cover design: Yakisha Simmons

Tiki Wadean Publishing

Life
cHanGers

Dedication To My Wife & Children

I want to dedicate this booklet to my wife of 25 years and my children who have supported me throughout the years of crisis and emotional challenges. My wife is a source of strength, encouragement and honesty which helped me to face and confront some of what I labeled "failures", but she labeled "learning experiences". Thank you sweetheart for being my pillar of strength and my pillow of rest. I love you with all of my heart; and you have surpassed all expectations as a woman of God, a wife, mother and friend. You gave me three awesome, anointed and loving children. Wayne, DeAndra and Tiffany, thank you for being the greatest gift a father could ever ask for. You watched and experienced many of my challenges, but you never complained during those challenging times. I love you so much.

Acknowledgments

I would like to acknowledge some people who have helped me, prayed for me and encouraged me during some difficult times:

- *To Evangelist Josephine Woodson*, a Godly woman who loves me unconditionally as a natural son. Thank you for your unwavering love and support. I love you, Momma!

- *To my spiritual dad, Apostle Herb Bright*, who took me in as a son when I felt fatherless. His love, compassion, teachings and trust in me helped me as a man and as a leader. He showed me that disagreeing with a decision doesn't mean you have to be unsupportive.

- *To my sisters, Natalie and Stacey*, my love for you will never die.

- *To Overseer Bonnie Bigelow and Elder Elvis Bigelow.* Thank you for coming into my life to help bring forth God's best for me in this season. Your family adopted us and made us a part of the family. God has great things in store for you.

- *To my publisher and editor, Yakisha Simmons* for encouraging me to pursue one of my dreams of writing this book. Your support and guidance during this process has helped me to continue to pursue more writings. Thank you and I love you, Cousin.

Introduction

The world is constantly and swiftly evolving daily. Everything that is made today will be obsolete tomorrow. Who is on top of the world tonight, could very well be on the opposite hemisphere by the dawn of the next day. Someone is always looking to outdo the other. To stay competitive, many of us are constantly on the go, on our cell phones and laptops, because we do not want to feel left behind in this information age. Social media has taken the place of human interaction and we are slowly losing the ability to personally communicate with each other effectively. This lack of human interaction has ultimately carried over into our spiritual lives where we no longer have time to stop, think, pray and trust. In other words, there is little to no relationship or communion with God.

Luke 18:1

And he spake a parable unto them to this end, that men ought always to pray, and not to faint.

Luke 18:1 of the King James Bible reminds us that men should always pray. Unfortunately, in this age of technology and less face to face contact, we have lost the ability to communicate effectively. Now, if God is not found on our iPhone© or

laptop, we very well may not communicate with Him at all.

Our days start with everything else except prayer and communion with God. We struggle repeatedly with the same issues because the only time we really talk to God is when we bless our food or when we mumble a few words just before falling off to sleep at night. Besides that, we do not take the necessary time to speak to God…to communicate… to develop a relationship… to stop, think, pray and trust.

What a difference it would make in our lives if we developed a pattern of communion with God. How much better would our lives be if we had a direct and uninterrupted connection with the God who has our steps purposefully ordered? What issues and hurts could we leave behind if we developed a relationship with the healer of all diseases?

This book was written to help you reach your God given potential. It will help you develop that essential relationship with the Father. It will help to heal some old wounds from the past, give you the tools to forgive and put you on a pathway forward.

The solution is to allow God to become the first order of our day. Before we get caught up in the hustle and bustle of life, we must stop and pray.

Stop, Think, Pray, Trust

The first 20 minutes of your day can set the tone for your entire day. I made it easy for you to get started. If you just pick up this booklet every day when you awake before you do anything else, it will help you have a positive start to your day. Each segment is divided into four sections of five minutes each: **STOP, THINK, PRAY** and **TRUST** and should only take approximately 20 minutes to complete. Of course, you are not limited to 20 minutes. As you develop a consistent prayer and meditation routine, you may find yourself spending more and more time with God. My recommendation is that you set your alarm to get up 20 minutes earlier than you usually do. This will give you a cushion of time and eliminate any need for you to rush through your meditation. Do this every morning and you will find yourself desiring more of God and enjoying a more peaceful and fulfilling day.

I. Minutes One to Five

Don't check voicemail, email or snail mail. *Don't* turn on the television or radio to access the news of the day. Take time to be still and invite the Lord into your morning.

> *Stand in awe, and sin not: commune with your own heart upon your bed, and be still. Selah.*
>
> *Psalm 4:4*

STOP

Every morning our minds are inundated with chatter about what we need to get done, who we have to see and where we have to go. We spend our entire morning planning how we are going to accomplish our goals and handle the people and situations of the day. Don't pre-plan, predict or pre-arrange anything about your day. Before the order of your day starts, stop and be still. Prepare yourself to commune with the Lord.

If you have already started doing things this morning, STOP now. Prepare now to get your thoughts in order. Relax and empty your mind. Dump anxiety about the full day ahead; release yesterday… it's over now; discard those old wounds.

Exercise forgiveness for things and people that may have hurt or hindered you. What happened yesterday is now over and you cannot go back to change it. This will become easier each day as you start to put your thoughts in order.

Scripture References

Be still, and know that I am God: I will be exalted among the heathen, I will be exalted in the earth.

Psalm 46:10

And let the peace of God rule in your hearts, to the which also ye are called in one body; and be ye thankful.

Colossians 3:15

And he arose, and rebuked the wind, and said unto the sea, Peace, be still. And the wind ceased, and there was a great calm.

Mark 4:39

And the peace of God, which passeth all understanding, shall keep your hearts and minds through Christ Jesus.

Philippians 4:7

II. Minutes Five to Ten

Take time to think about what God has already done in your life. Think about your successes and even your failures. Think of who He is to you and what He has done for you. What do you want to accomplish with God's help? Order your thought process for the day!

When your day starts with bad news, your mood will be reflective of what you allowed your mind and spirit to feed upon when you arose.

THINK

Finally, brethren, whatsoever things are true, whatsoever things are honest, whatsoever things are just, whatsoever things are pure, whatsoever things are lovely, whatsoever things are of good report; if there be any virtue, and if there be any praise, think on these things.

Philippians 4:8

We are faced with the negative things of this world every day and whether directly or indirectly, those things have an effect on our thoughts. If we are not careful, our minds can become inundated with images of death, destruction and crime which create negative memories and ultimately alters our spirit. All of these negative images will have an effect on your day. You will find yourself reflecting all day on the negative images you have seen and the negative sounds you have heard, which will produce negative interactions.

Don't just start your day with positive thinking, but also with positive actions. Do and/or say something positive to yourself, family members and even friends. Once you have finished your 20 minutes, tell someone else to have a blessed day or tell them how much you love and appreciate them. Teach them this 20 minute principle.

I realize, because of how cynical many of us have become and how much hurt we may have suffered, starting this process can prove to be challenging. However, when you start your day with positive spiritual thinking and positive actions, even if your day doesn't go according to plans, your actions will reflect your thoughts and God will provide you an

Philippians 4:7

And the peace of God, which passeth all understanding, shall keep your hearts and minds through Christ Jesus.

Colossians 3:15

And let the peace of God rule in your hearts, to the which also ye are called in one body; and be ye thankful.

With the scriptures and the peace of God in your spirit and mind, you will make it through the day and have the ability to accomplish successes throughout your day.

inner peace that will surpass your own understanding.

    This step is crucial to your starting your day. Once you stop and prepare your spirit for meditation, flood your thoughts with those that are good. Allow positive images and messages to replay in your mind. All that is lovely, good and pure… think on those things. Darkness is chased away when light makes its grand entrance. Don't let darkness linger there in the threshold of your thoughts. Chase them away with the light. This will only contribute to your having a more positive day.

Scripture References

And be not conformed to this world: but be ye transformed by the renewing of your mind, that ye may prove what is that good, and acceptable, and perfect, will of God.

Romans 12:2

For as he thinketh in his heart, so is he:

Proverbs 23:7

And now, dear brothers and sisters, one final thing. *Fix your thoughts* on what is true, and honorable, and right, and pure, and lovely, and admirable. Think about things that are excellent and worthy of praise.

Philippians 4:8 (NLT)

III. Minutes Ten to Fifteen

Before starting your day, you remembered to STOP everything you started and you have thought on everything that God has done for you; even the challenges He's helped you through. Now, it is time to pray and commune with the Lord. Before you pray, you must believe that the Lord hears you and that He will receive your prayers.

PRAY

The Lord hath heard my supplication; the Lord will receive my prayer.
                                        Psalm 6:9

For he that cometh to God must believe that He is, and that He is a rewarder of them that diligently seek him.
                                        Hebrews 11:6b

What is prayer? Prayer is a conversation with God. It is an opportunity for you to speak to Him and Him to you. A couple that does not communicate will eventually grow apart. Or if their communication is ineffective, the bonds of union will start to wither.

There are many perceptions and misconceptions about prayer and if God even hears them. I can assure you, He does. He longs to commune with you so that the bonds of His union with you can be restored or strengthened.

Many of you probably feel that you do not have time to do this every day; however, I encourage you to make time to order your day. Start your day with order... God's order... God first. Seek Him diligently and when you start your day with God, everything that was meant for an evil purpose, God will use it to bring good to you and He will get the glory out of your day.

Scripture References

Be careful for nothing; but in everything by prayer and supplication with thanksgiving let your requests be made known unto God.

Philippians 4:6

And he spake a parable unto them to this end, that men ought always to pray, and not to faint;

Luke 18:1

Pray without ceasing.

1 Thessalonians 5:17

If my people, which are called by my name, shall humble themselves, and pray, and seek my face, and turn from their wicked ways; then will I hear from heaven, and will forgive their sin, and will heal their land.

2 Chronicles 7:14

IV. Minutes Fifteen to Twenty

TRUST

One of life's greatest challenges, I have found through my own personal experiences, is the ability to trust. Trusting others can be a challenge; but we can even doubt our own selves at times because of external forces that shaped our way of thinking.

For example, during an incredibly crucial time in my life when I was growing into a young man and maturing, I was criticized by my parents and other family members concerning some life choices I made. Being a young man and growing up the way that I did, I was bound to make some choices of which my parents would not agree. The problem was not the choices that I made, but the repeated reminder of the choice.

No matter what I did, I was constantly told, "That was a bad decision" or "You should not have done it that way." Every decision was based on "what others would think" and the negative affect on others more so than the positive benefit a decision may have had on me. They highlighted all of the negative reactions of others, especially church people, and repeated their negative comments. Unfortunately, all of that negativity was improperly projected on to me. So, after years and years of that, I became a people pleaser, began to distrust my own ability to make decisions as an adult and made decisions about me based on the opinions and feelings of family and church people.

What I have come to understand is that my parents and family members were inadvertently using this method to keep me emotionally and physically tied to them. I was an intricate part of the church; so, because of my position, I was manipulated into staying around even when I felt it was time to go. I was told that it would be wrong for me to leave because it would destroy my father's dreams. I could not pursue my own dreams because my father's dream was more important. That was unfortunate and rather unhealthy; but, it was done to us possibly because it was done to them, not necessarily by their parents, but perhaps by their own spiritual leaders.

Have you ever wondered why you always needed someone else's approval for a decision that you have made or were about to make? Take a look at your past. Were you encouraged to make your own decisions? Were your dreams nurtured or hampered? Were you criticized or celebrated? Were you shaped to value other's opinions of you or to be bold and proud of the person that is you who was fearfully and wonderfully made? Were you taught to fly or were your wings clipped at an early age? Were demands placed on you for the sake of image?

Don't get me wrong, it is okay to seek sound advice and wise counsel; however, don't let that advice become a sign of approval or disapproval regarding your own decisions. Although this was my experience, through time, I had to let those negative memories go and learn to trust the God in me for myself.

Whatever you're holding on to, you must release. Let go of those negative memories and experiences. Don't get stuck where you are. You must believe in yourself and remember that the steps of a good man are ordered by the Lord. With God all things are possible; so, you can only trust yourself when you have God in you leading and guiding you through this journey. This is not to say that you have never made a bad decision on your own or will not make any more in the future. Though your environment shaped and formed you, does not mean it will have to dictate your future.

Take some time now to affirm to yourself, and do this daily, "Decisions I make today will bring me success and not failure." Continue to speak positive words regarding your future, discard negative comments past or present, and trust in the Lord with all of your heart. For if you trust in Him with all of your heart, he will make your pathway clear.

Trust in the Lord with all thine heart,
and lean not unto thine own understanding.
In all thy ways acknowledge him,
and he shall direct thy paths.

Proverbs 3:5-6

As you are ordering your day, through prayer, ask Him to direct your path as your day is being planned. Ask God to help you in your decision-making processes. Ask Him to guide you. There are three scripture verses I love that remind us to trust in The Lord and also to do good things. There is a reward and that reward is success!

> *Trust in the LORD, and do good; so shalt thou dwell in the land, and verily thou shalt be fed. Delight thyself also in the LORD; and he shall give thee the desires of thine heart. Commit thy way unto the LORD; trust also in him; and he shall bring it to pass.*
>
> *Psalm 37:3-5*

Scripture References

The God of my rock; in him will I trust: he is my shield, and the horn of my salvation, my high tower, and my refuge, my saviour; thou savest me from violence.

2 Samuel 22:3

The Lord is my rock, and my fortress, and my deliverer; my God, my strength, in whom I will trust; my buckler, and the horn of my salvation, and my high tower.

Psalm 18:2

O Lord of hosts, blessed is the man that trusteth in thee.

Psalm 84:12

As for God, his way is perfect; the word of the Lord is tried: he is a buckler to all them that trust in him.

2 Samuel 22:31

Conclusion

Keep in mind twenty minutes is not an absolute time frame, but a starting point for you. I am sure after you start this process, the time allotted for each principle will increase as you grow deeper in Him. The goal is to get started which can prove most challenging, but YOU CAN DO IT!

This material is not purposed to just be an exercise; it is intended to help you start a lifetime of order for the start of your day. As you read every scripture, allow it to be absorbed into your mind, soul and spirit. The Lord will make your way *and* your day prosperous!

This book of the law shall not depart out of thy mouth; but thou shalt meditate therein day and night, that thou mayest observe to do according to all that is written therein: for then thou shalt make thy way prosperous, and then thou shalt have good success.

Have not I commanded thee? Be strong and of a good courage; be not afraid, neither be thou dismayed: for the LORD thy God is with thee whithersoever thou goest.

Joshua 1:8-9

Everything that is in your thoughts and heart to do for success today, the Lord is with you. Believe in yourself and trust God to help you make sound life decisions. If by any chance you make a decision that's unfavorable to you, forgive yourself, learn from your mistake and quickly move on. Don't dwell in a place of self-deprecating and failure. When you are faced with a challenge, allow the peace of God to rule in you. Affirm to yourself daily that your day and your life *will* be better because of God's order. Let God continue to heal you and show you direction.

About the Author

W. A. Simmons was born on July 22, 1961 to the late Bishop Nathaniel and Johnnie Mae Simmons. He served in ministry with his parents since the age of three years old as a drummer, playing in revivals led by his father and grandfather. At the age of eleven, God anointed his hands and he started to learn how to play the organ. At Zion Chapel Fire Baptized Holiness (F.B.H) Church, Chicago, Illinois, W. A. Simmons practiced for hours every day as he prayed for God to anoint his hands. Being told many times that his playing was not suitable for the services, he kept practicing and playing. After about two years of devotion to the craft, God honored his prayers and he became an anointed and renowned organist, requested by many to play in different venues and churches.

Because of his gift, he was the organist for his father's church in Chicago, Illinois and later in Newark, New Jersey. At the beginning stages of the ministry in Newark, the windows were raised during the summer to allow the praises of God and the sound of the music to go out. The melodious sounds of praise and worship reached into the park across the street. Of those who visited and subsequently received Christ as their savior, the majority's testimony was that they were drawn in by the sound of the music. During that time, the church there in Newark grew from 13 members to over 900 over the course of the next few years.

W. A. Simmons, like many young men upon reaching a certain age, tried to spread his wings seeking to leave home to attend college and/or experience military life. However, he was discouraged by his parents who stated he should not pursue his own interests because he was there to help his father in ministry. His role there was more important and, therefore, required his complete attention. So, he played for every choir, every rehearsal and every service for many years and without compensation.

In 1987, after being ordained an Elder in the F.B.H. Church, he felt that it was time to move on. So, he relocated to Charlotte, NC where he married the love of his life, Kim, now of 25 years. From this union, God blessed them with three wonderful, anointed children who continue to support him without being coaxed or manipulated. In 1988, he met Bishop H.L. Bright, Sr. and God led him to become a part of Faith Tabernacle Outreach Ministries. It was during these years that he was mentored by, now his spiritual father, H. L. Bright, Sr. and elevated to various offices due to the anointing on his life and his unwavering commitment to God and ministry.

W. A. Simmons attended Phoenix University from 2005-2007 and is currently enrolled at Broward College where he is completing a Bachelor of Science degree in Information Technology. He currently resides in the state of Florida where he's building a ministry for the Kingdom.

www.ingramcontent.com/pod-product-compliance
Lightning Source LLC
Chambersburg PA
CBHW070951040426

42443CB00012B/3301